POETRY FROM THE MOVIE

Grace
WINS

Apostle Linda Sweezer-Rowster

AuthorHouse™
1663 Liberty Drive
Bloomington, IN 47403
www.authorhouse.com
Phone: 833-262-8899

This book is printed on acid-free paper.

ISBN: 979-8-8230-1274-4 (sc)
ISBN: 979-8-8230-1276-8 (hc)
ISBN: 979-8-8230-1275-1 (e)

Library of Congress Control Number: 2023914531

Print information available on the last page.

Published by AuthorHouse 08/09/2023

authorHOUSE®

POEMS

Darkness and Confusion

Darkness and Confusion seems

Inevitable wherever I trod

Receiving nothing from anyone

Not even a recognized nod

This struggle that I have faced

From year after year

Has made me starkly bitter

Not feeling anyone near

I lost my Mom to domestic violence

My Dad never stopped his hurt

He drove her into a storm

He led her to the dirt

What do you do, realistically

When Failure is your name

Not sure of your Inside

Just playing the world's game

You do whatever you can

To pacify that drought

You understand, from all fronts

There is unquestionably, no way out

This Darkness

This darkness that's over me

Is trying to take my life

I can't wake up again tomorrow

So full of sadness and strife

I've got to meliorate myself

I have to find my way through

I WILL stop my comfort method

God, I don't need you.

It's Obvious to me...

It's obvious to me right now

That I can't do this alone

The will to do it in my flesh

Has caused me further to moan

Mama, you told me to trust Him

To receive His GIFT of grace

I see now that when I DO YIELD

He Inarguably sets the PACE

Mom you gave me the gift of poetry

A way to express my heart

Now I run back to His GRACE

That brings me out the dark

Freedom

Saved by His Mercy, kept by His love

What a Joy to Taste

JESUS' wonder through the Dove

The Holy Spirit has divulged to me

The Depth of His Grace

It does not matter how far you fall

You land succinctly in His Face

It cannot be earned, nor merited

Nor is it deserved at all

He gives it to His children by Faith

A Remedy from THE FALL

How Cruel

How cruel the Day that I was Born

A life full of Struggle, Failure and Scorn

Why me, I cried but no Reply

Like my Mother, I wanted to Die

Why did my Mother, so kind and meek

Meet someone who knocked her off her feet

She gave him all, he took her life

My life, the picture now of hurt and strife

What do you do, where do you go??

God, I need some help, I want to know

I keep trying, but I keep failing,

Nothing's changing, so much railing

A Glimmer of Hope

A glimmer of Hope, I may survive

It looks like the shore is now on my side

I walked with just instincts, now I see

That you really do have a PLAN for Me

I see just a flicker, but it's coming my way

So dark was the night, now a glimpse into the Day

This addiction was arresting and holding me tight

But My mom told me once, "Jesus gets it right!"

Grace was Enough

Jesus made it to the finish line

His Grace WAS enough

I tried to do it all

Yes, I tried to be so tough

I analyzed the Grace Message

To see just how I fit

I found that Grace

Not only saves us

But puts us in Jesus' niche

So all this time that I wasted

Thinking that I didn't count

Kept me from experiencing

The Power of Jesus' Mount

Confusion

What's wrong with me, now
Can't detain my thoughts
Feel so unproductive
I know it's my own fault

Come back to me creativity
No time for you to roam
I need to help myself
To arrive at the dome

The Trauma of Transition

The trauma of transition
Has gripped my very heart
I felt that I was at the finish line
But was only again at start

This darkness is so cloudy
I can't see my way through
Don't know who will win
Me or GRACE YOU

Hurting you is inevitable
If I stay and hold you close
For I am still bewildered,
Let me suffer the most.

I must protect you from me
My path is still uncertain
Not sure yet of myself
Will He roll back my curtain?

I still must distance myself
And watch my steps, my pace
Still uncertain if I'll Win
But knowing I need His Grace

Inside Me

Inside me is the Damaged Place
Pursuing me, A derailed Train
It appears no help for me in sight
My Mind so consumed with Pain

How can such damage ever be fixed
How can this derailing end
I tried, to operate on myself
To Help my vexations mend

I found out distinctly, from my falls
That Self-Effort never wins
Divine Support and Healing
Causes the status to bend

Damage is your Specialty Jesus
You know how to make us again
Thank you, my Grace Savior
Thank you, my Powerful Friend.

It doesn't matter how hopeless it is
It doesn't matter the view
Your Grace has the Ethereal Power
To make everything about us NEW

QUESTIONS

What do you do?
When the tide seems to shift
And normalcy is gone
Suddenly your life is changed
And your spirit seems to roam

Where do you go?
When the mirror is not fair
It shows you only a streak
You don't like what you perceive
Not envisioning what to seek

How do you maneuver?
When nothing seems to move
Because the guilt and frustration
Has taken away your groove

Life seems so unreasonable
When you feel so all alone
When no one understands you
That makes you joyless-prone

God's Place

By Apostle Linda Sweezer Rowster

There Is A Place Of Solace,

So high above the hills,

A place of GREAT PEACE,

That defies the human will.

Jesus has a LOVE and Joy,

That captures the heart of Man,

Reach out and Embrace His Song,

As only a BELIEVER can.

This book contains most of the poetry from my movie: Grace Wins.

In the movie, the main character, Brian, encounters massive storms in his life due to being a victim/survivor of Domestic Violence. We have captured the feelings from those moments in the movie. I have also included some Domestic Violence Prevention Tips for those who may not be aware of the subtlety of them.

This poetry is germane to understanding the impact of what happens in a home of Domestic Violence as it pertains to even the children. This movie highlights a Poet who wrote during his trying times and includes the majority of the poems that he recites in Grace Wins. I have included a personal narrative, from my perspective, concerning underlying life lessons about Domestic Violence. The main character, Brian, was, along with his mother, a victim and a survivor of Domestic Violence.

The information that I am sharing has come from my backgrounds as a licensed Social Worker for 16 years, my own personal experiences, and my work, for almost 30 years as a licensed and ordained Minister of the Gospel of Jesus Christ. It is a life- threatening crime that has a pattern of red-flags that go along with it. I would like to begin by giving you a definition of Domestic Violence. It affects millions of individuals across the United States regardless of age, race, religion, economic status, gender, sexual orientation or educational background. We are tuned in to it many times after high- profile cases come to light. After then, we forget that Domestic Violence happens to someone EVERY DAY.

According to the statistics from the National Coalition Against Domestic Violence(NCADV):

- On average, nearly 20 people per minute are physically abused by an intimate partner in the United States. During one year, this equates to more than 10 million women and men.

- 1 in 4 women and 1 in 9 men experience severe intimate partner physical violence, intimate partner contact sexual violence, and/or intimate partner stalking with impacts such as injury, fearfulness, post-traumatic stress disorder, use of victim services, contraction of sexually transmitted diseases, etc.

- 1 in 3 women and 1 in 4 men have experienced some form of physical violence by an intimate partner. This includes a range of behaviors (e.g. slapping, shoving, pushing) and in some cases might not be considered "domestic violence."

- 1 in 7 women and 1 in 25 men have been injured by an intimate partner.

- 1 in 10 women have been raped by an intimate partner. Data is unavailable on male victims.

- 1 in 4 women and 1 in 7 men have been victims of severe physical violence (e.g. beating, burning, strangling) by an intimate partner in their lifetime.

- 1 in 7 women and 1 in 18 men have been stalked by an intimate partner during their lifetime to the point in which they felt very fearful or believed that they or someone close to them would be harmed or killed.

- On a typical day, there are more than 20,000 phone calls placed to domestic violence hotlines nationwide.

- The presence of a gun in a domestic violence situation increases the risk of homicide by 500%.

- Intimate partner violence accounts for 15% of all violent crime.

- Women between the ages of 18-24 are most commonly abused by an intimate partner.

- 19% of domestic violence involves a weapon.

Sources:

[1] Catalano, S., U.S. Bureau of Justice Statistics. Special Report: Intimate Partner Violence, 1998-2010. (Nov. 2012, revised Sep. 2015)

[2] Tjaden, P., and Thoennes, N., U.S. Department of Justice. Extent, Nature, and Consequences of Intimate Partner Violence. (July 2000).

[3] Centers for Disease Control and Prevention, "The National Intimate Partner and Sexual Violence Survey: 2010 Findings on Victimization by Sexual Orientation," 2013.

[4] Centers for Disease Control and Prevention, "The National Intimate Partner and Sexual Violence Survey: 2010 Findings on Victimization by Sexual Orientation," 2013.

There are many types of abuse but mental and emotional abuse generally begins the cycle or pattern. Sexual and financial abuse enter in and then many times, the physical abuse begins or escalates. There is not a definite pattern to when the manifold abuse happens. It happens quickly in some relationships and in others it slowly develops. I want you to understand that threats are also forms of abuse because they are generally signals that more abuse is coming.

Here are some of the Red Flags that I have seen as I counseled many from the ages of 15 to 45 that have been common and recognizable patterns.

1. The individual's POWER is taken away. Their control is also gone.

2. The perpetrator blames the victim for everything and takes no responsibility for their behavior.

3. Perpetrator brings in dishonest "baggage" from their previous relationship (s) to justify how they were mis-treated by blaming the former partners.

4. Perpetrator operates the relationship in extreme jealousy. Acts as if they don't trust the one who is victimized. Sometimes this is a red flag of infidelity on their part.

5. The victim has to tell the perpetrator where they are at all times. Perpetrator even stalks the job site of the victim.

6. Perpetrator causes low self-esteem in the victim by saying that they are unattractive and dumb.

7. Perpetrator also criticizes and condemns those who have been positive motivators in the victim's inner circle. The goal is to move everyone out of your circle but him.

What Keeps the Victim there? Here are only some of the reasons

1. The perpetrator has succeeded in removing the positive support system and has them in isolation.

2. Being embarrassed or ashamed to tell anyone.

3. The victim's life and many times the children's lives are threatened. There is a real threat of death.

4. An emotional tactic called gaslighting, helps the perpetrator to cause the victim to feel like they are responsible for the abuse. It is used to confuse and shift blame onto the victim. This often causes the victim to doubt their mental capacity and feel like they are responsible for the abuse and therefore able to stop it by doing what the perpetrator says. This rarely happens.

5. Waiting on the perpetrator to change. Many say that they will not do it again but they do.

6. The victim is not financially able to live on their own.

There Is Help:

Survivors have many options, Call the local Police Department. Get some documentation on file…PLEASE FOLLOW UP when your case comes to court. You may also obtain a protection order from your local court and/stay in a shelter. There is hope for victims, and they are not alone. Let's also SPEAK UP TO THE LOCAL LAW ENFORCEMENT FOR OTHERS WHO CANNOT FIND THEIR VOICES.

Finally:

If you are in danger, call a local hotline, the National Domestic Violence Hotline, or, if it is safe to do so, 911.

- The National Domestic Violence Hotline provides confidential and anonymous support 24/7. Reach out by phone at 1-800-799-7233 and TTY 1-800-787-3224.

- Loveisrespect provides teens and young adults confidential and anonymous support. Reach out by phone 1-866-331-9474 and TTY 1-866-331-8453.

- WomensLaw.org provides legal information and resources for victims. Reach out by email through the WomensLaw Email Hotline in English and Spanish.

Apostle Linda Sweezer-Rowster

Biography

Humble Beginnings & Family

Apostle Linda Sweezer-Rowster is the Founder and Senior Pastor of the House of Peace Worship Church International. She is married to First Man Timothy Rowster and has two children: Prophet Anthony Sweezer and Prophetess Ann Sweezer. She is the Proud Grandmother of Harmonie Sweezer.

Born the tenth child to the late Bessie Dillard and the late Alfred Dillard, Jr. in Vicksburg, Mississippi, she was saved at the tender age of ten. She was called into the Gospel Ministry on February 5, 1995; ordained in 1997; and ordained again in 2006 by Bishop T.D. Jakes of Dallas, Texas at The Potter's House International. She was called to Pastor, and Founded *"The House of Peace Worship Church"* in December 2001. In 2006, she planted a second location of the Church in Rolling Fork, MS. The third location Church was planted in Atlanta, GA, in 2015. HOPis known as "the Church Where the Holy Spirit is in Charge."

On July 23, 2011, she was affirmed and consecrated as an Apostle.

Education & Accomplishments

Apostle received her Bachelors degree in English with a minor in Political Science from Millsaps College in Jackson, MS.

She holds a Doctorate Degree in Theology. A playwright for over forty years, she has written, produced and directed sixteen major productions. She is the author of a book entitled, "Eating Along the Way!" A Survivor's Guide for People Who are Serious About Hearing God's Call.

Since 2015, Apostle Sweezer-Rowster has been operating *Grace Through Faith School of Ministry*. It is a school of Theology where her Teaching Gift of the Five-Fold Ministry Gifts flows freely. The school operates year-round, is open to the public via virtual registration and offers various levels of degrees, from Certificates to Bachelor to Doctorate degrees.

She is the CEO of The Peace Place Counseling Services, the Director of the House of Peace Feeding and Tutoring Program in Vicksburg and Rolling Fork, and the former owner of the Peaceful Place Daycare and After School program.

Awards, Recognitions, Certifications & Civic Achievements

In November 2018, she received the "Women Empowering Communities Ministry Leader Award by Mountain of Faith Ministries. In 2017, she was awarded the Dr. Martin Luther King Jr. "Pioneer of the Dream Award" and is a one of the Founding Members (33 years) of the Rev. Dr. Martin Luther King, Jr. Memorial Day Committee. Other achievements include recognition by the Honorable Benny G. Thompson, US Representative, and listed in the Congressional Record and proceedings of the 114th United States Congress. In 2022, she received The Voice Award and the Celebrate Her Award.

Appointed Board Member of the United Way of West Central Mississippi (2011-2014), Former Director of The House of Peace Substance Abuse Prevention Program, and Appointed to the Election Commission from 2005 to 2020. In 2021, she was elected as Case Manager for the Municipal Domestic Violence Court and elected to the Board of the Mississippi Coalition Against Domestic Violence.

Apostle Sweezer-Rowster is a member of Mu Xi Omega Chapter of Alpha Kappa Alpha Sorority, Inc., a former member of the Mission Mississippi Pastoral Alliance; two times appointed to the City of Vicksburg Civil Service Commission; A licensed Social Worker for sixteen years; Chosen by the Ivyettes of Alpha Kappa Alpha Sorority, Inc. as one of the Religious Role Models; Outstanding Young Women of America; Woman of Excellence Award in Art and Literature; honored as a Local Recipient of 100 Black Women; Recognized as a Distinguished African-American by St. Mark Freewill Baptist Church; Nominated as one of the 50 Leading Business Women of America; A scholarship was given in her name by Alpha Phi Alpha Fraternity at the Dr. Martin Luther King, Jr. Breakfast; Appointed to the Vicksburg Warren School District Advisory Council. She is a former member of the Board of Directors for WWISCAA (Warren Washington Issaquena Sharkey Community Action Agency).

Apostle's Favorite Scripture: "I can do all things through Christ which strengthened me." Philippians 4:13

Printed in the United States
by Baker & Taylor Publisher Services